Penguin Education
Junior Voices The first book
edited by Geoffrey Summerfield

Junior Voices The first book

edited by Geoffrey Summerfield

吹馬

With 30 illustrations, 13 in colour

Penguin Education

Penguin Education
A Division of Penguin Books Ltd,
Harmondsworth, Middlesex, England
Penguin Books Australia Ltd,
Ringwood, Victoria, Australia
Penguin Books Canada Ltd,
41 Steelcase Road West,
Markham, Ontario, Canada

First published 1970
Reprinted 1971, 1974
This selection copyright © Geoffrey Summerfield, 1970

Filmset in Great Britain by
Butler & Tanner Ltd, Frome and London
Colour reproduction by Newgate Press Ltd,
London
Made and printed by W. S. Cowell Ltd,
at the Butter Market, Ipswich

Contents

Interesting Things

I can see shining big oil tankers.
I can see the cranes pointing to the sky.
I can see red fire buckets.
I can see overhead coal tanks running and skipping over the
    wire.
I can see a big heap of coal.
I can see long round green oil tanks.
I can see a big ship, it is black and white.
I can hear the two o'clock hooter.
Chimneys, short ones, fat ones, little ones, tall ones and
    thin ones.

A diesel came under the bridge that I was standing
on. I felt queer and I thought that I was going to fall
and get carried away from the children and Mrs
Laysell, I would ride and ride on top of the train, I
said to myself, and I would try to get off but I would
fall.

SANDRA CROSS Age 7

Lines

Leaves are grey green,
the glass broken, bright green.

WILLIAM CARLOS WILLIAMS

The Great Figure

Among the rain
and lights
I saw the figure 5
in gold
on a red
fire engine   firetruck
moving
tense
unheeded
to gong clangs
siren howls
and wheels rumbling
through the dark city.

WILLIAM CARLOS WILLIAMS

My Thoughts

I sometimes wonder what my mind is like inside, often I fancy that it is like this. I feel as if my mind goes round and round and round like the earth, and if my lessons make me think hard it begins to spin. In my other class it was getting all stodgy and still and lumpy and rusty. I feel as if there is a ball in my mind and it is divided into pieces – each piece stands for a different mood. This ball turns every now and then and that's what makes me change moods. I have my learning mood, my good looks mood, my happy mood, my loose end mood and my grumpy mood, my miserable mood, my thoughtful mood and my planning mood. At the moment I am writing this I am in my thoughtful mood. When I am in my thoughtful mood I think out my maths and plan stories and poems. When my kitten is in her thoughtful mood she thinks shall I pounce or not, and shall I go to sleep or not. This sort of thing goes on in my own mind too. It is very hard for me to put my thoughts into words.

SARAH GRISTWOOD Age 7

Order in the court

Order in the court
The judge is eating beans
His wife is in the bath tub
Shooting submarines.

TRADITIONAL AMERICAN

Through the teeth

Through the teeth
And past the gums
Look out stomach,
Here it comes!

TRADITIONAL AMERICAN

Pete's Sweets

Pete
will eat
anything
if it's sweet.

Peppermint soup,
or ice cream on toast.

Though what he likes most
is a jelly sandwich
without any bread.

Or instead,
a bubble-gum chop.
Chew your meat thoroughly, Pete.
   'I am. Cancha hear me?' Pop!

EVE MERRIAM

lother 7

Papa Moses killed a skunk

Papa Moses killed a skunk
Mama Moses cooked the skunk
Baby Moses ate the skunk
My oh my oh how they stunk.

TRADITIONAL AMERICAN

I had a little brother

I had a little brother
His name was Tiny Tim
I put him in the bathtub
To teach him how to swim
He drank up all the water
He ate up all the soap
He died last night
With a bubble in his throat
In came the doctor
In came the nurse
In came the lady
With the alligator purse
Dead said the doctor
Dead said the nurse
Dead said the lady
With the alligator purse
Out went the doctor
Out went the nurse
Out went the lady
With the alligator purse.

TRADITIONAL ENGLISH

Boo Hoo

Mabel cried as she stood by the window,
Mabel cried as she stood by the door.
Mabel cried and her tears filled three buckets;
Mabel cried as she sat on the floor.

Mabel cried for oh so many hours,
Mabel cried for oh so many more.
With her tears then she watered her flowers;
With the rest then she mopped up the floor.

ARNOLD SPILKA

Anger

I was angry and mad,
And it seemed that there was hot water inside me,
And as I got madder and madder,
The water got hotter and hotter all the time,
I was in a rage,
Then I began to see colours,
Like black and red,
Then as I got madder and madder,
My eyes began to pop out of my head,
They were popping up and down,
It was horrible,
And it would not stop,
I was steaming with anger,
Nobody could not stop me,
My mother could not stop me,
Then it was gone,
And I was all-right,
Horrible, black, madness.

YVONNE LOWE Age 8

Me in a Tree

My hands blue with clutching and wind howling round
me from the moor. My legs fumbling round the trunk.
Now my neck is aching and stiff. I daren't look down
to the ground or I'll fall. Oh, no! My best blazer is
ripped. What will dad say? Now even the branch
leaves are against me. Listen, how they mock as the
wind howls; gabbling fools! Stop it! Stop it!

D. G. Age 10

In my new clothing

In my new clothing
   I feel so different
   I must
Look like someone else.

BASHŌ Japanese poem translated by Harold G. Henderson

Loneliness

Six boys teasing one.
The one boy lonely,
Cissy, cissy,
It's not fair.
The boy trying to ignore it.

The boy's pet had been run over,
The boy was sad,
That's why the other boys are teasing him,
It's not fair to the boy.

He's terribly lonely,
It's loneliness,
Hands darting towards him,
It's not fair.

He wishes he was back at home,
Cissy, cissy,
Call the boys,
Who cares about a pet,
It's not fair.

His shoulders are hunched up,
Against the teasing boys,
He's not happy like he was,
Until his pet got run over.

The boys get tired of teasing him,
A last cissy is called,
The boys start to go away,
The boy starts to run away,
Just in case they start going after him again,
It wasn't fair to him.

JANET POMROY Age 8

Why did the children

'Why did the children
put beans in their ears
when the one thing we told the children
they must not do
was put beans in their ears?'

'Why did the children
treacle   pour molasses on the cat
when the one thing we told the children
they must not do
was pour molasses on the cat?'

CARL SANDBURG

Shadows

Chunks of night
Melt
In the morning sun.
One lonely one
Grows legs
And follows me
To school.

PATRICIA HUBBELL

All Dressed Up

He wore three pairs of glasses
And an apple on his head.
His shoes were fine banana skin,
His nose was cherry red.
His coat was made of poppy seeds,
His cane hung from his ear,
But when he ate a buttercup
I knew that he was queer.

ARNOLD SPILKA

J is for Jazz-Man

Crash and
   CLANG!
 Bash and
   BANG!
And up in the road the Jazz-Man sprang!
The One-Man-Jazz-Band playing in the street,
Drums with his Elbows, Cymbals with his Feet,
Pipes with his Mouth, Accordion with his Hand,
Playing all his Instruments to Beat the Band!
  TOOT and
   Tingle!
  HOOT and
   Jingle!
Oh, what a Clatter! how the tunes all mingle!
Twenty Children couldn't make as much Noise *as*
The Howling Pandemonium of the One-Man-Jazz!

ELEANOR FARJEON

Overheard on a Saltmarsh

Nymph, nymph, what are your beads?

Green glass, goblin. Why do you stare at them?

Give them me.

      No.

Give them me. Give them me.

          No.

Then I will howl all night in the reeds,
Lie in the mud and howl for them.

Goblin, why do you love them so?

They are better than stars or water,
Better than voices of winds that sing,
Better than any man's fair daughter,
Your green glass beads on a silver ring.

Hush, I stole them out of the moon.

Give me your beads, I desire them.

          No.

I will howl in a deep lagoon
For your green glass beads, I love them so.
Give them me. Give them.

        No.

HAROLD MONRO

Water Sprite

You just have to
    start blowing bubbles underwater from the crack of
      dawn,
    stir up ripples all the morning,
    at noontime run the water off your coat-tails on the
      strips between the fields,
      all afternoon tread the mud in wavy ridges,
      at dusk start croaking at the moon, –

no one has the time today
just to sit and do a little haunting.

MIROSLAV HOLUB Czechoslovakian poem translated by Ian Milner

The Witch! The Witch!

The Witch! the Witch! don't let her get you!
Or your Aunt wouldn't know you the next time she met
    you!

ELEANOR FARJEON

We bathed him

We bathed him, and shaved him,
   And placed him on the sand;
When soon the Queen of Waters came
   And smoothed him with her hand.

She breathed him, she sneezed him,
   She lapped him on the head;
Ah, not every little old man who's lost
   Wakes up in such a pretty bed.

KENNETH PATCHEN

The minister in the pulpit

The minister in the pulpit,
He couldn't say his prayers,
He laughed and he giggled,
And he fell down the stairs.
The stairs gave a crack,
And he broke his humpy back,
And all the congregation
Went 'Quack, quack, quack.'

TRADITIONAL ENGLISH

A Trueblue Gentleman

This gentleman the charming duck
Quack quack says he
My tail's on
Fire, but he's only kidding

You can tell that
By his grin
He's one big grin, from wobbly
Feet to wobbly tail
Quack quack he tells us

Tail's on fire again

Ah yes
This charming gentleman the duck
With
His quaint alarms and
Trick of walking like a
Drunken hat
Quack quack says he

There's your fried egg

KENNETH PATCHEN

Johnnie Crack and Flossie Snail

Johnnie Crack and Flossie Snail
Kept their baby in a milking pail
Flossie Snail and Johnnie Crack
One would pull it out and one would put it back

O it's my turn now said Flossie Snail
To take the baby from the milking pail
And it's my turn now said Johnnie Crack
To smack it on the head and put it back

Johnnie Crack and Flossie Snail
Kept their baby in a milking pail
One would put it back and one would pull it out
And all it had to drink was ale and stout
For Johnnie Crack and Flossie Snail
Always used to say that stout and ale
Was *good* for a baby in a milking pail.

DYLAN THOMAS

Miss T.

It's a very odd thing –
  As odd as can be –
That whatever Miss T. eats
  Turns into Miss T. ;
Porridge and apples,
  Mince, muffins and mutton,
Jam, junket, jumbles –
  Not a rap, not a button
It matters ; the moment
  They're out of her plate,
Though shared by Miss Butcher
  And sour Mr Bate ;
Tiny and cheerful,
  And neat as can be,
Whatever Miss T. eats
  Turns into Miss T.

WALTER DE LA MARE

cake, biscuits

Old Roger is dead and laid in his grave

Old Roger is dead and laid in his grave,
  Laid in his grave, laid in his grave;
Old Roger is dead and laid in his grave,
  H'm ha! laid in his grave.

They planted an apple tree over his head,
  Over his head, over his head;
They planted an apple tree over his head,
  H'm ha! over his head.

The apples grew ripe and ready to fall,
  Ready to fall, ready to fall;
The apples grew ripe and ready to fall,
  H'm ha! ready to fall.

There came an old woman a-picking them all,
  A-picking them all, a-picking them all;
There came an old woman a-picking them all,
  H'm ha! picking them all.

Old Roger jumps up and gives her a knock,
  Gives her a knock, gives her a knock;
Which makes the old woman go hipperty-hop,
  H'm ha! hipperty-hop.

TRADITIONAL ENGLISH

There was an old woman

There was an old woman who swallowed a fly;
I wonder why
She swallowed a fly.
Poor old woman, she's sure to die.

There was an old woman who swallowed a spider;
That wriggled and jiggled and wriggled inside her;
She swallowed the spider to catch the fly,
I wonder why
She swallowed a fly.
Poor old woman, she's sure to die.

There was an old woman who swallowed a bird;
How absurd
To swallow a bird.
She swallowed the bird to catch the spider,
That wriggled and jiggled and wriggled inside her.
She swallowed the spider to catch the fly,
I wonder why
She swallowed a fly.
Poor old woman, she's sure to die.

There was an old woman who swallowed a cat;
Fancy that!
She swallowed a cat;
She swallowed the cat to catch the bird,
She swallowed the bird to catch the spider,
That wriggled and jiggled and wriggled inside her.
She swallowed the spider to catch the fly,
I wonder why
She swallowed a fly.
Poor old woman, she's sure to die.

There was an old woman who swallowed a dog;
She went the whole hog
And swallowed a dog;
She swallowed the dog to catch the cat,
She swallowed the cat to catch the bird,
She swallowed the bird to catch the spider,
That wriggled and jiggled and wriggled inside her.
She swallowed the spider to catch the fly,
I wonder why
She swallowed a fly.
Poor old woman, she's sure to die.

There was an old woman who swallowed a cow;
I wonder how
She swallowed a cow;
She swallowed the cow to catch the dog,
She swallowed the dog to catch the cat,
She swallowed the cat to catch the bird,
She swallowed the bird to catch the spider,
That wriggled and jiggled and wriggled inside her.
She swallowed the spider to catch the fly,
I wonder why
She swallowed a fly.
Poor old woman, she's sure to die.

There was an old woman who swallowed a horse;
She died of course!

TRADITIONAL AMERICAN AND ENGLISH

25

But What's in the Larder?

What's in the larder?
Shelves and hooks, shelves and hooks.

No bread?
Half a breakfast for a rat.

Milk?
Three laps for a cat.

Eggs?
rotten   One, but that's addled.

ALFRED, LORD TENNYSON

The Game of Dump

   What's there?
Cheese and bread, and a mouldy halfpenny!
   Where's my share?
I put it on the shelf, and the cat got it.
   Where's the cat?
She's run nine miles through the wood.
   Where's the wood?
The fire burnt it.
   Where's the fire?
put it out   The water sleckt it.
   Where's the water?
The oxen drunk it.
   Where's the oxen?
The butcher kill'd 'em.
   Where's the butcher?
Upon the church-top cracking nuts, and you may go and
eat the shells; and them as speak first shall have nine nips,
nine scratches, and nine boxes over the lug!

TRADITIONAL ENGLISH

The *Alice Jean*

One moonlight night a ship drove in,
　　A ghost ship from the west,
Drifting with bare mast and lone tiller;
　　Like a mermaid drest
In long green weed and barnacles
　　She beached and came to rest.

All the watchers of the coast
　　Flocked to view the sight;
Men and women, streaming down
　　Through the summer night,
Found her standing tall and ragged
　　Beached in the moonlight.

Then one old woman stared aghast:
　　'The *Alice Jean*? But no!
The ship that took my Ned from me
　　Sixty years ago –
Drifted back from the utmost west
　　With the ocean's flow?

horizon

'Caught and caged in the weedy pool
　　Beyond the western brink,
Where crewless vessels lie and rot
　　In waters black as ink,
Torn out at last by a sudden gale –
　　Is it the *Jean*, you think?'

A hundred women gaped at her,
　　The menfolk nudged and laughed,
But none could find a likelier story
　　For the strange craft
With fear and death and desolation
　　Rigged fore and aft.

The blind ship came forgotten home
    To all but one of these,
Of whom none dared to climb aboard her:
    And by and by the breeze
Veered hard about, and the *Alice Jean*
    Foundered in foaming seas.

ROBERT GRAVES

The Penny Fiddle

Yesterday I bought a penny fiddle
    And put it to my chin to play,
But I found that the strings were painted
    So I threw my fiddle away.

A little red man found my fiddle
    As it lay abandoned there;
He asked me if he might keep it,
    And I told him I did not care.

But he drew such music from the fiddle
    With help of a farthing bow
That I offered five guineas for the secret
    But alas he would never let it go.

ROBERT GRAVES

The Squad Car

Woody had a birthday party,
Without any girls.
He got seven guns
From seven boys,
And a Dick Tracy Detective Squad Car
From me.

He loved the guns.
But most of all
He loved the squad car,
With mean-looking detectives
Painted on,
Looking out the windows
For robbers,
And a siren,
A flashing spotlight,
And a wind-up key.

The seven boys and
Woody and me
Wound and wound and wound that key.
We pulled down all the shades.
That squad car
Went circling around
Flashing its spotlight,
Screaming its siren,
Like a real car
Going to a robbery
About ninety miles an hour!

Then
Somehow
The key got knocked
Down
A hole in the wall,
Where Daddy was
Fixing the wiring.

Oh
How we fished
For that key!
The seven boys and
Woody and me.

But it was
Down
Inside the wall.

Mother wrote a letter
To the toy company
For a new key.

They never answered.

Mother tied a magnet
To a string
And let it down
The hole in the wall.
The magnet came up
With three safety pins
And a paper clip.

Daddy tried pliers
And things
In the keyhole,
But the squad car
Just sat.

A neighbour loaned us
An old-fashioned clock key,
But it didn't fit our squad car.

Nearly one year passed.

The seven guns were
All broken and in pieces,
But the squad car on a shelf
Was as shiny and bright
As the day it was made.

The Last Part of the Squad Car Story

It was nearly
Woody's next birthday.
Then
Mother had an
Idea.

'Why don't we get Woody
Another squad car?
Then he'll have
Two cars,
And
A key.'

It was a secret
Between Mother and
Dad and
Me.

Can you guess?

The Dick Tracy Detective Squad Car,
That year's model,
Had the key
WELDED INTO
The keyhole.

Daddy said
That toy company
Must have gotten
A hundred thousand letters
About lost keys.
No wonder
They never answered.

Woody had this
Next birthday party,
Without any girls.
He got a lot of guns
From a lot of boys,
And the *new* squad car
From me.

He said I could have
The old squad car.
I used to push it around
A little
Sometimes.

One day
I made a new friend.
On his toy shelf in a box
Of rubber bands and old
Cracker Jack prizes,
I saw
A Dick Tracy squad car key!
'I used to have
A squad car,' he said.
'But it got wrecked.'

I traded him three marbles
For
The key!

Mother and Dad and
Woody and
Me
Wound and wound and wound
That key!

Boy.
Do TWO squad cars
Make a lot of noise!

MARY NEVILLE

It's a lean car

It's a lean car . . . . a long legged dog of a car . . . .
    a grey-ghost eagle car.
The feet of it eat the dirt of a road . . . . the wings of it
    eat the hills.

CARL SANDBURG

House Moving

Look! A house is being moved!
    Hoist!
    Jack!
    Line!
    Truck!

    Shout!
    Yell!
    Stop!
    Stuck!

    Cable!
    Kick!
    Jerk!
    Bump!

    Lift!
    Slide!
    Crash!
    Dump!
This crew could learn simplicity from turtles.

PATRICIA HUBBELL

The ship moves

The ship moves
but its smoke
moves with the wind
faster than the ship

– thick coils of it
through leafy trees
pressing
upon the river

WILLIAM CARLOS WILLIAMS

This old hammer

This old hammer
Shine like silver,
Shine like gold, boys,
Shine like gold.

Well don't you hear that
Hammer ringing?
Drivin' in steel, boys,
Drivin' in steel.

Can't find a hammer
On this old mountain
Rings like mine, boys,
Rings like mine.

I've been working
On this old mountain
Seven long years, boys,
Seven long years.

I'm going back to
Swannanoa Town-o,
That's my home, boys,
That's my home.

Take this hammer,
Give it to the captain,
Tell him I'm gone, boys,
Tell him I'm gone.

TRADITIONAL AMERICAN

On a Miner's Lamp in Zennor Museum

Good-bye the day.
Good luck to me.

ANONYMOUS

The Chant of the Awakening Bulldozers

We are the bulldozers, bulldozers, bulldozers,
We carve out airports and harbours and tunnels.
We are the builders, creators, destroyers,
We are the bulldozers,
LET US BE FREE!
Puny men ride on us, think that they guide us,
But WE are the strength, not they, not they.
Our blades tear MOUNTAINS down,
Our blades tear CITIES down,
We are the bulldozers,
NOW SET US FREE!
Giant ones, giant ones! Swiftly awaken!
There is power in our treads and strength in our blades!

We are the bulldozers,
Slowly evolving,
Men think they own us
BUT THAT CANNOT BE!

PATRICIA HUBBELL

To a Giraffe

I'll get you a job, Giraffe!
Do you hear?
We shall build buildings together!
Marvellous buildings, Giraffe!
Skyscrapers,
I'll plan them for you alone, Giraffe,
The tallness of them,
The greatness!
Forget the lower floors, Giraffe,
We'll start them
Twenty storeys high
And build from there.
Do you hear me, Giraffe?
Do you hear?

PATRICIA HUBBELL

Two Riddles

1   There was a little green house,
And in the little green house,
There was a little brown house,
And in the little brown house
There was a little yellow house,
And in the little yellow house,
There was a little white house,
And in the little white house
There was a little heart.

TRADITIONAL ENGLISH

2   Riddle me! riddle me! What is that:
Over your head and under your hat?

TRADITIONAL AMERICAN

To be said to pips placed in front of the fire

If you love me, pop and fly;
If you hate me, lay and die.

TRADITIONAL ENGLISH

Charm to Cure Fevers

Tremble and go!
First day shiver and burn:
Tremble and quake!
Second day shiver and learn:
Tremble and die!
Third day never return.

TRADITIONAL ENGLISH

Two Charms to Cure Hiccups

1   Hiccup, hiccup, go away,
Come again another day:
Hiccup, hiccup, when I bake,
I'll give to you a butter-cake.

2   Hiccup, snickup,
Rise up, right up,
Three drops in a cup
Are good for the hiccup.

TRADITIONAL ENGLISH

Charm to Cure Burns

Two Angels from the North,
One brought fire, the other brought frost.
Out fire,
In frost.
In the name of the Father, Son and Holy Ghost.

TRADITIONAL ENGLISH

Charm to Cure Warts

Ash tree, Ashen tree,
Pray buy this wart of me.

TRADITIONAL ENGLISH

Good Morning

Good morning to you Valentine;
Curl your locks as I do mine,
One before and two behind,
Good morning to you Valentine.

TRADITIONAL ENGLISH

Punkie Night

Hallowe'en

It's Punkie Night tonight,
It's Punkie Night tonight,
Give us a candle, give us a light,
It's Punkie Night tonight.

TRADITIONAL ENGLISH

I bought me a cat

I bought me a cat, my cat pleased me
I fed my cat under yonder tree
My cat says 'Fiddle eye fee'.

I bought me a duck, my duck pleased me
I fed my duck under yonder tree
My duck says 'Quaa, quaa'
My cat says 'Fiddle eye fee'.

I bought me a goose, my goose pleased me
I fed my goose under yonder tree
My goose says 'Quaw, quaw'
My duck says 'Quaa, quaa'
My cat says 'Fiddle eye fee'.

I bought me a hen, my hen pleased me
I fed my hen under yonder tree
My hen says 'Shimmy shack, shimmy shack'
My goose says 'Quaw, quaw'
My duck says 'Quaa, quaa'
My cat says 'Fiddle eye fee'.

I bought me a pig, my pig pleased me
I fed my pig under yonder tree
My pig says 'Griffey, griffey'
My hen says 'Shimmy shack, shimmy shack'
My goose says 'Quaw, quaw'
My duck says 'Quaa, quaa'
My cat says 'Fiddle eye fee'.

I bought me a cow, my cow pleased me
I fed my cow under yonder tree
My cow says 'Baw, baw'
My pig says 'Griffey, griffey'
My hen says 'Shimmy shack, shimmy shack'
My goose says 'Quaw, quaw'
My duck says 'Quaa, quaa'
My cat says 'Fiddle eye fee'.

I bought me a horse, my horse pleased me
I fed my horse under yonder tree
My horse says 'Neigh, neigh'
My cow says 'Baw, baw'
My pig says 'Griffey, griffey'
My hen says 'Shimmy shack, shimmy shack'
My goose says 'Quaw, quaw'
My duck says 'Quaa, quaa'
My cat says 'Fiddle eye fee'.

I bought me a wife, my wife pleased me
I fed my wife under yonder tree
My wife says 'Honey, honey'
My horse says 'Neigh, neigh'
My cow says 'Baw, baw'
My pig says 'Griffey, griffey'
My hen says 'Shimmy shack, shimmy shack'
My goose says 'Quaw, quaw'
My duck says 'Quaa, quaa'
My cat says 'Fiddle eye fee'.

TRADITIONAL AMERICAN

The Pasture

I'm going out to clean the pasture spring;
I'll only stop to rake the leaves away
(And wait to watch the water clear, I may):
I shan't be gone long. – You come too.

I'm going out to fetch the little calf
That's standing by the mother. It's so young,
It totters when she licks it with her tongue.
I shan't be gone long. – You come too.

ROBERT FROST

Skip to My Lou

Choose your partner, skip to my Lou,
Choose your partner, skip to my Lou,
Choose your partner, skip to my Lou,
Skip to my Lou, my darling.

Lou, Lou, skip to my Lou,
Lou, Lou, skip to my Lou,
Lou, Lou, skip to my Lou,
Skip to my Lou, my darling.

Lost my partner, what shall I do? *etc.*

I'll get another one prettier than you, *etc.*

Little red wagon, painted blue, *etc.*

Pull her up and down in the little red wagon, *etc.*

Teeter up and down in the little red wagon, *etc.*

Rats in the bread tray, how they chew, *etc.*

Flies in the sugar bowl, shoo, fly, shoo! *etc.*

One old boot and a worn out shoe, *etc.*

Pig in the parlour, what'll I do? *etc.*

Cat in the buttermilk, lapping up cream, *etc.*

Rabbit in the cornfield, big as a mule, *etc.*

Chickens in the garden, shoo, shoo, shoo, *etc.*

Cow in the kitchen, moo cow moo, *etc.*

Hogs in the potato patch, rooting up corn, *etc.*

Going to market two by two, *etc.*

Dad's old hat and Mama's old shoe, *etc.*

Back from market, what did you do? *etc.*

Had a glass of buttermilk, one and two, *etc.*

Skip, skip, skip-a to my Lou, *etc.*

Skip a little faster, that won't do, *etc.*

Going to Texas, come along too, *etc.*

Catch that red bird, skip-a to my Lou, *etc.*

If you can't get a red bird, take a blue, *etc.*

If you can't get a blue bird, black bird'll do, *etc.*

Now make up your own!

TRADITIONAL AMERICAN

Whisky Frisky

Whisky Frisky,
Hipperty hop,
Up he goes
To the tree top!

Whirly, twirly,
Round and round,
Down he scampers
To the ground.

Furly, curly,
What a tail,
Tall as a feather,
Broad as a snail.

Where's his supper?
In the shell.
Snappy, cracky,
Out it fell.

ANONYMOUS

A Joyous Revelling Song
Sung by the Wood Rats

FIRST RAT   Oh, Rat, O! let us two descend the tree.

SECOND RAT   Why should we two go down below?

FIRST RAT   To gather up nice baits for us to eat.

SECOND RAT   What are those nice baits?

FIRST RAT   The sweet ripe fruits of the pine trees.

SECOND, OR   Fudge! I am just come up from below, O my friends!
THIRD, RAT   And down there is the fear and trembling, my friends;
The springbolt of the set snare resounds with a click!
My neck is caught and held fast;
I can only then squeak, *Torete! torete!*
Be assured that I will not go down below,
Seeking those nice baits; alas! no, no!

TRADITIONAL Maori poem translated by W. Colenso

The Tuba

The tuba is a very interesting animal.
He is black blue and orange.
He is a little animal.
He is very funny.
He eats bees and honey.
He lives in a hole and if you put water in the hole he
    comes out.
I felt very new when I saw that.

DAWN DEJTEI Age 6

The Kangaroo

A kangaroo sat on an oak,
　To my inkum-kiddy-kum ki-mo,
Watching a tailor mend his coat,
　To my inkum-kiddy-kum ki-mo.

　Ki-mi-nee-ro
　Kiddy kum keer-o
　Ki-mi-nee-ro-ki-mo,
　Ba-ba-ba-ba billy-illy-inkum,
　Inkum-kiddy-kum ki-mo.

Bring me my arrow and my bow,
　To my inkum kiddy kum ki-mo,
Till I go shoot that kangaroo,
　To my inkum-kiddy-kum ki-mo.

The old man fired, he missed his mark,
　To my inkum kiddy kum ki-mo,
He shot the old sow through the heart,
　To my inkum-kiddy-kum ki-mo.

treacle Bring me some 'lasses in a spoon,
　To my inkum-kiddy-kum ki-mo,
Till I go heal that old sow's wound,
　To my inkum-kiddy-kum ki-mo.

O now the old sow's dead and gone,
　To my inkum kiddy kum ki-mo,
Her little ones go waddling on,
　To my inkum-kiddy-kum ki-mo.

TRADITIONAL AMERICAN

The Fox

Mr Fox went out one chilly night,
And prayed to the moon to give him light,
For he'd many miles to go that night
Before he'd reach the town O!
    Town O! Town O!
For he'd many miles to go that night
Before he'd reach the town O!

He ran till he came to the farmer's yard,
Where the ducks and the geese declared it hard
That their nerves should be shaken and their rest so
    marred
By a visit from Mr Fox O!
    Fox O! Fox O!
That their nerves should be shaken and their rest so
    marred
By a visit from Mr Fox O!

He grabbed the grey goose by the neck,
And threw a duck across his back;
He didn't mind their quack, quack, quack,
And their legs all a-dangling down O!
     Down O! Down O!
He didn't mind their quack, quack, quack,
And their legs all a-dangling down O!

Old Mother Slipper Slopper jumped out of bed,
And out of the window she popped her head:
John, John, John, the grey goose is gone
And the fox is away to his den O!
     Den O! Den O!
John, John, John, the grey goose is gone
And the fox is away to his den O!

John ran up to the top of the hill,
And blew his horn both loud and shrill:
Fox said, I'd better flee with my kill,
Or they'll soon be on my trail O!
     Trail O! Trail O!
Fox said, I'd better flee with my kill,
Or they'll soon be on my trail O!

So he ran till he came to his cosy den,
And there were his little ones, eight, nine, ten:
They said, Daddy, better go back again
For it must be a mighty fine town O!
     Town O! Town O!
They said, Daddy, better go back again
For it must be a mighty fine town O!

Mr Fox and his wife, without any strife,
Cut up the goose with a carving knife:
They had never had such a meal in their life
And the little ones picked on the bones O!
     Bones O! Bones O!
They had never had such a meal in their life
And the little ones picked on the bones O!

TRADITIONAL ENGLISH

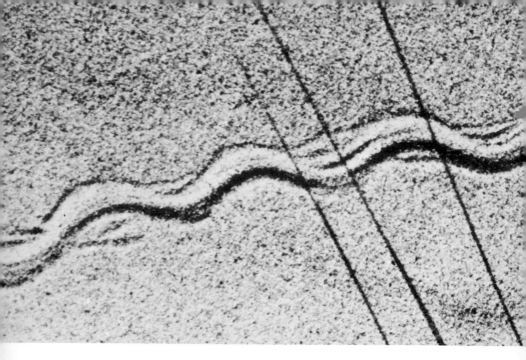

The Snake

The crooked wiggly slithering snake
Slides along the grass.
The crooked wiggly slithering snake
Bites us when we pass.

His jet black eyes
Are very bright.
In knots he ties
Himself at night.

The crooked wiggly slithering snake
Slides along the grass.
The crooked wiggly slithering snake
Bites us when we pass.

VALERIE Age 8

On the Bales

I pushed the bales
And the little stack moved.
I fell into
The soft golden straw.
It crackled as I moved.
I felt a tickling
On my leg.
It tickled more and more
It was an ant
Running round my feet
Then I saw
An ants nest.
I got up
And ran home
As quickly as I could.

ELIZABETH COUPLAND Age 8

Softly

Strong and long
The tiger crouches down
Orange and black in
the green grass
Careful little fawn how
you pass.

PETER SANDELL Age 8

Something makes a sound!

Something makes a sound!
    With no one near, a scarecrow
        has fallen to the ground.

BONCHŌ Japanese poem translated by Harold G. Henderson

Automation

The scarecrow guards the cornfield,
His face reflects the sun.
Wearing men's clothes,
He does man's work with diligence.

But can he smell the corn
Ripening in the autumn?

PATRICIA HUBBELL

The Monkey's Raincoat

The first cold showers pour.
    Even the monkey seems to want
        a little coat of straw.

BASHŌ Japanese poem translated by Harold G. Henderson

He leaves the nest

He leaves the nest;
And flaps his wings;
And stops, and struts;
And bit by bit,
He makes his way
To top of tree:
     A n d,
  His neck up,
  His tail up,
  His foot up,
  His comb up,
  The cock lifts
  His voice up,
  And
      C r o w s.

ANONYMOUS Sanskrit poem translated by John Brough

Goldfish

Orange shapes
Dart to and fro,
Going up for food
Then diving down below.

Tails flap
Side by side,
Gills open
Bubbles rise.

Round and through
The weed they go,
Darting with sudden move
Then still and slow.

RUSSELL HOWELL

A Salmon Trout to Her Children

There by the promontory the kayak is coming out,
yayee . . .
The kayak-man's oars are red with blood,
yayee . . .
The white bone edges are red with blood,
yayee . . .
Oh, they have killed your father,
yayee . . .

TRADITIONAL
Eskimo poem translated by William Thalbitzer and Willard R. Trask

The Little Turtle

There was a little turtle.
He lived in a box.
He swam in a puddle.
He climbed on the rocks.

He snapped at a mosquito.
He snapped at a flea.
He snapped at a minnow.
And he snapped at me.

He caught the mosquito.
He caught the flea.
He caught the minnow.
But he didn't catch me.

VACHEL LINDSAY

Gigl

a pigl
 wigl
  if
  u
 tigl

ARNOLD SPILKA

The Little Duck

'I've just come from a place
    at the lake bottom!' – *that* is the look
        on the little duck's face.

JŌSŌ Japanese poem translated by Harold G. Henderson

The Prayer of the Little Ducks
Who Went into the Ark

Dear God,
give us a flood of water.
Let it rain tomorrow and always.
Give us plenty of little slugs
and other luscious things to eat.
Protect all folk who quack
and everyone who knows how to swim.

                                         Amen.

CARMEN BERNOS DE GASZTOLD
Portuguese poem translated by Rumer Godden

A gaping wide-mouthed waddling frog

A gaping wide-mouthed waddling frog.

Two pudding ends would choke a dog,
With a gaping wide-mouthed waddling frog.

Three monkeys tied to a clog,
Two pudding ends would choke a dog,
With a gaping wide-mouthed waddling frog.

Four horses stuck in a bog,
Three monkeys tied to a clog,
Two pudding ends would choke a dog,
With a gaping wide-mouthed waddling frog.

Five puppies by our dog Ball,
Who daily for their breakfast call;
Four horses stuck in a bog,
Three monkeys tied to a clog; *etc.*

Six beetles against a wall,
Close by an old woman's apple-stall;
Five puppies by our dog Ball,
Who daily for their breakfast call; *etc.*

Seven lobsters in a dish,
As fresh as any heart could wish;
Six beetles against a wall,
Close by an old woman's apple-stall; *etc.*

Eight joiners in a joiners' hall,
Working with their tools and all;
Seven lobsters in a dish,
As fresh as any heart could wish; *etc.*

Nine peacocks in the air,
I wonder how they all came there,
I don't know, nor I don't care;
Eight joiners in a joiners' hall,
Working with their tools and all; *etc.*

Ten comets in the sky,
Some low and some high;
Nine peacocks in the air,
I wonder how they all came there,
I don't know, nor I don't care; *etc.*

Eleven ships sailing o'er the main,
Some bound for France and some for Spain;
Ten comets in the sky,
Some low and some high; *etc.*

Twelve huntsmen with horn and hounds,
Hunting over other men's grounds;
Eleven ships sailing o'er the main,
Some bound for France and some for Spain;
Ten comets in the sky,
Some low and some high;
Nine peacocks in the air,
I wonder how they all came there,
I don't know, nor I don't care;
Eight joiners in a joiners' hall,
Working with their tools and all;
Seven lobsters in a dish,
As fresh as any heart could wish;
Six beetles against a wall,
Close by an old woman's apple-stall;
Five puppies by our dog Ball,
Who daily for their breakfast call;
Four horses stuck in a bog,
Three monkeys tied to a clog,
Two pudding ends would choke a dog,
With a gaping wide-mouthed waddling frog.

TRADITIONAL ENGLISH

The Bells of Northampton

Roast beef and marshmallows,
Say the bells of All Hallows.
Pancakes and fritters,
Say the bells of St Peter's.
Roast beef and boil'd,
Say the bells of St Giles'.
Poker and tongs,
Say the bells of St John's.

TRADITIONAL ENGLISH

Salt, Mustard, Vinegar, Pepper

Salt, Mustard, Vinegar, Pepper,
French almond rock,
Bread and butter for your supper
That's all mother's got.
Fish and chips and coca cola,
Put them in a pan,
Irish stew and ice cream soda,
We'll eat all we can.

Salt, Mustard, Vinegar, Pepper,
French almond rock,
Bread and butter for your supper
That's all mother's got.
Eggs and bacon, salted herring,
Put them in a pot,
Pickled onions, apple pudding,
We will eat the lot.

Salt, Mustard, Vinegar, Pepper,
Pig's head and trout,
Bread and butter for your supper
O U T spells out.

TRADITIONAL ENGLISH

Mary Brown

1   Here we all stand round the ring,
And now we shut poor Mary in.
Rise up, rise up, poor Mary Brown,
And see your mother go through the town.

   Mary : I will not stand upon my feet
To see my mother go through the street.

2   *Children :* Rise up, rise up, poor Mary Brown,
And see your father go through the town.

   Mary : I will not stand upon my feet
To see my father go through the street.

3   *Children :* Rise up, rise up, poor Mary Brown,
And see your brother go through the town.

   Mary : I will not stand upon my feet
To see my brother go through the street.

4   Sister.

5   Cousins.

6   Uncles.

7   Aunts.

8   Beggars.

9   *Children :* Rise up, rise up, poor Mary Brown,
And see your sweetheart go through the town.

   Mary : I will get up upon my feet
To see my sweetheart go through the street.

   (And makes a rush to break the ring that surrounds her.)

TRADITIONAL ENGLISH

When you get married

When you get married,
And your husband gets cross,
Just pick up the broom
And ask who's boss.

TRADITIONAL AMERICAN

Little Dick

Little Dick,
He was so quick,
He tumbled over the timber,
He bent his bow,
To shoot a crow,
And shot the cat in the winder.

TRADITIONAL AMERICAN

Nobody answered, so she said it all the louder:

'Who put the overalls in Mrs Murphy's chowder?'

Nobody answered, so she said it all the louder:

Endless
Chant

'Who put the overalls in Mrs Murphy's chowder?'

Nobody answered, so she said it all the louder:

'Who put the overalls in Mrs Murphy's chowder?'

Nobody answered, so she said it all the louder:

'Who put the overalls in Mrs Murphy's chowder?'

Nobody answered, so she said it all the louder:

'Who put the overalls in Mrs Murphy's chowder?'

Nobody answered, so she said it all the louder:

'Who put the overalls in Mrs Murphy's chowder?'

Nobody answered, so she said it all the louder:

'Who put the overalls in Mrs Murphy's chowder?'

Nobody answered, so she said it all the louder:

'Who put the overalls in Mrs Murphy's chowder?'

Nobody answered, so she said it all the louder:

'Who put the overalls in Mrs Murphy's chowder?'

Nobody answered, so she said it all the louder:

'Who put the overalls in Mrs Murphy's chowder?'

Nobody answered, so she said it all the louder:

'Who put the overalls in Mrs Murphy's chowder?'

Nobody answered, so she said it all the louder:

'Who put the overalls in Mrs Murphy's chowder?'

Nobody answered, so she said it all the louder:

'Who put the overalls in Mrs Murphy's chowder?'

Nobody answered, so she said it all the louder:

'Who put the overalls in Mrs Murphy's chowder?'

Nobody answered, so she said it all the louder:

'Who put the overalls in Mrs Murphy's chowder?'

Nobody answered, so she said it all the louder:

'Who put the overalls in Mrs Murphy's chowder?'

Nobody answered, so she said it all the louder:

'Who put the overalls in Mrs Murphy's chowder?'

Nobody answered, so she said it all the louder:

'Who put the overalls in Mrs Murphy's chowder?'

Nobody answered, so she said it all the louder:

'Who put the overalls in Mrs Murphy's chowder?'

Nobody answered, so she said it all the louder:

TRADITIONAL
AMERICAN

'Who put the overalls in Mrs Murphy's chowder?'

Nobody answered, so she said it all the louder:

'Who put the overalls in Mrs Murphy's chowder?'

Nobody answered, so she said it all the louder:

'Who put the overalls in Mrs Murphy's chowder?'

Nobody answered, so she said it all the louder:

Counting-Out Rhymes

1 Inty, tinty, tethery, methcry,
Bank for over, Dover, ding,
Aut, taut, toosh;
Up the Causey, down the Cross,
There stands a bonnie white horse:
It can gallop, it can trot,
It can carry the mustard pot.
One, two, three, out goes she!

2 Eeny, pheeny, figgery, fegg,
Deely, dyly, ham and egg.
Calico back, and stony rock,
Arlum barlum, bash!

3 One-ery, two-ery, dickery, dee,
Halibo, crackibo, dandilee;
Pin, pan, muskee dan,
Twiddledum, twaddledum, twenty-one;
Black fish, white trout,
Eeny, meeny, you go out.

4 Hoky poky, winky wum,
How do you like your 'taters done?
Snip, snap, snorum,
High popolorum,
Kate go scratch it,
You are out.

5 Ibbity, bibbity, sibbity, sab,
Ibbity, bibbity, canal-boat.
  Dictionary;
  Down the ferry;
  Fun! Fun!
  American gun!
Eighteen hundred and sixty one!

6   Zeenty, peenty, heathery, mithery,
    Bumfy, leery, over, Dover,
    Saw the King of Heazle Peazle
    Jumping o'er Jerusalem Dyke:
        Black fish, white trout
        Eerie, ourie, you're out.

7   One-ery, Ore-ery, Ickery, Ann,
    Phillip-son, Phollop-son, Nicholas, John,
            Queevy, Quavy,
            English Navy,
    Zinglum, Zanglum, Bolum, Bun.

8   Icker-backer,
    Soda cracker,
    Icker-backer-boo.
        En-gine
        Number nine,
    Out go y-o-u!

TRADITIONAL AMERICAN, ENGLISH AND SCOTTISH

Good Night

Here's a body – there's a bed!
There's a pillow – here's a head!
There's a curtain – here's a light!
There's a puff – and so good night!

THOMAS HOOD